LovE-mail

LovE-mail

Romantic Messages for Lovers

Herman Gould and Marge C. Gould

Writer's Showcase

San Jose New York Lincoln Shanghai

LovE-mail
Romantic Messages for Lovers

Writer's Showcase
an imprint of iUniverse.com, Inc.

For information address:
iUniverse.com, Inc.
5220 S 16th, Ste. 200
Lincoln, NE 68512
www.iuniverse.com

ISBN: 0-595-20006-0

Printed in the United States of America

Contents

Preface

The words, *You've Got Mail,* have had a very special romantic meaning for us since we met on America Online. Right from the first day when we communicated online, we began getting to know one another through email messages, which, after meeting face to face, quickly became daily expressions of love.

Because these electronic affirmations of love have had such a significant impact on our relationship, we have continued sending them daily throughout our courtship and romance. Even though we have a very rich and full life, and are both very successful in our careers, Marge, as a teacher/ author, and Herman, as a doctor of optometry, we have found that receiving a love e-mail message from one another is one of our most treasured moments we experience each day.

E-mail has become an extremely popular means of communication for millions of people, but very few ever think to send e-mail messages of love to their partners.

We have written this book to encourage others to use their home computers and e-mail as a means of reaffirming their love for their partners and for enhancing their relationships on a daily basis.

This little book is a literary gift of love for both men and women who would like to add some romance to their relationships with their spouses, partners, or lovers.

The lines on every page are expressed with deep love, and you will find that they represent many themes and life's experiences and events which will have some meaning or relevance to your own life. There is a message for every day of the year, and several additional ones to get you started on a second year and inspire you to create your own unique love e-mail messages for the special person in your life.

They are there for the taking in any manner you choose. They may be incorporated into your personal love e-mail message, or they may be used to inspire your own creativity in writing your own original love e-mail messages. They may simply be read and shared with your partner.

In whatever way you and your loved one choose to use the LovE-mail messages contained in this little book, we hope they will contribute to continually renewing your love for one another and to keeping your relationship and your love fresh, exciting, and fulfilling.

Herman Gould
Marge Christensen Gould

Section 1

Love Messages for
Every Day of the Year

1. Rhapsody of Love
I want you to continually feel an inner contentment with my love that is reaffirmed with the rhythm of your breathing and the tempo of your heartbeat. My mission is for us to resonate in a rhapsody of love.

2. Oneness
The oneness of the love we share is a treasure that will always remain sacred and protected in my heart.

3. Tapestry
Prior to falling in love with you, my life was like viewing the reverse side of a tapestry. Once we discovered our love for one another, the tapestry turned itself around, as did my life, and the full harmony of the colors, the intricacies of the patterns and the beauty of the fabric became vibrant and meaningful.

4. Flavor of Life
You have converted my life from dull to dynamic. You have added flavorings and seasonings of companionship, devotion, adoration, and true love to the ingredients of my existence. I savor the flavor of life that you have placed before me.

5. Memory
In my muscle memory, I sense the feel of your body in my arms, the thrill of your kiss, and the warmth of your touch. In my heart memory, I delight in your affirmations of love, expressions of contentment, and promises of joy everlasting.

6. Designers of Our Future
We are truly blessed as the designers and architects of the blueprints of our future. We are genuinely one on the path into all of our tomorrows. I love you dearly and deeply, and repeatedly express my gratitude to you for being you.

7. Illuminated
You have illuminated my life and transported me from the mundane to the magnificent. You cause my attitude to be buoyant and my life to be bountiful.

8. Liberated

You have liberated my spirits, restoring my life's equilibrium with the promise of serene tomorrows. That serenity is built on a firm foundation of mutual love.

9. Tapestry of Love

You are the golden thread and I am the silver filament that are woven together to create our tapestry of love. I love the exquisite fabric of the life we have created together.

10. Passion

Have I told you lately how much I love you? Do you have a deep awareness of the intensity of my love, my affection, my caring, and my passion for you?

11. Highest Calling

Do you know that my highest calling is pleasing you and making you happy? I have made satisfying you and creating a wonderful life for us my personal mission.

12. Precious
To be loved by someone whom you love is a most precious gift. Love given and returned is the highest form of spirituality.

13. Essence
As I wander from room to room in our home, I sense your essence clinging to the items in each room, constantly reminding me of you. This gives me a tremendous feeling of inner peace and great contentment.

14. Textures of Life
You have taken the fibers and textures of life and harmonized them into a magnificent tapestry that is our life together. The passion of the creator of life's tapestry is manifested in our love.

15. Marvelous Fit
How can it be explained that we are such a marvelous fit? We match in every detail—our minds and our bodies, our goals and our dreams, our desires and our eagerness.

16. Love is an Action Word

I bring you this message of love and devotion to nourish our togetherness. We are agreed that Love is a verb—an action word. I desire to put as much loving action as possible into our relationship. By my actions, I want to demonstrate the intensity of my love for you.

17. Reassuring Rhythms of My Life

I treasure the reassuring rhythms of my life: your laugh, your breathing at night, the words, "I love you," your touch, your footsteps, your voice on the telephone, the motion of our dancing and holding each other tightly.

18. Delight

I delight in our embraces and the passion in our kisses and hugs. You are vital to my peace of mind and sense of well-being.

19. Our Life Together

Our life together is beautiful and filled with deep love and fulfillment. I will always treasure you. Together we are better and stronger than we are separately.

20. Love is a Continual Process
We both know that love is a continual process of honoring, sharing, respecting, touching, feeling, and serving each other. I will always work toward that goal.

21. Center of My Universe
You have become the very center of my universe—the most important and valued person in my life. My mind is filled with thoughts of you and of us together.

22. State of Bliss
You have brought me into a state of bliss that surmounts anything I had ever experienced or imagined in my entire life.

23. Our Love
You expand my heart, allowing more love to enter my body and reside there permanently. You are beautiful, and our intimacies give me great joy. Our love promises us marvelous possibilities. I treasure our love and all of our tomorrows.

24. Puzzle Pieces

We fit together like two puzzle pieces, formed of the same mold. There will never be a more fitting match than you and I. We are one.

25. Constantly Aware of My Love

With words of affection, squeezable hugs, tender touches, and acts of service, I want to make you constantly aware of my love.

26. Asset

Your love is the most important gift that I possess and I treasure it, will nurture it, and keep it in a safe place in my heart.

27. Treasure

I went on a treasure hunt and discovered you. What a treasure you are! I love you so very much.

28. Inner Reservoir of Love
I have an inner reservoir filled with an unending flow of love that will surround and nurture our marriage and this union.

29. Reassuring Ritual
Saying "I LOVE YOU," is a reassuring ritual that affirms our love, our togetherness, and our vows.

30. Inspiration
You are fantastic and are a true inspiration to me. You have provided me with the power of joy and helped me to find my true place in the universe.

31. Illuminating My Path
As we go hand in hand, and heart to heart, you are illuminating my path into the future. I love you dearly and deeply.

32. Rebirth of Spirit
Thank you, my darling, for being the catalyst of my love and the rebirth of my spirit. You enlighten my heart and renew my enthusiasm for life.

33. Pathway of Romance
You and I are on the pathway of romance that will be life-long. From here to there we will honor each other, strive for happiness, and explore the magnificence loving one another.

34. Rejoice
When I am with you, all is right with my world. You give me reason to rejoice, and make my dreams merge with my reality.

35. Emotional Bank Account
Here is something you can deposit in your personal emotional bank account, and that is the knowledge that my love for you is sincere and everlasting.

36. Pathways
We are truly in the same place, at the same time, facing in the same direction, and headed toward the same pathways. It is truly marvelous!

37. Facets
Our love is like the facets of a treasured diamond, each aspect reflecting the light differently and the brilliance dazzling the eye of the beholder.

38. Whispers of Imagination
Whispers of imagination motivate us to create a love and a life for ourselves that far exceeds our dreams and our visions.

39. Microcosm
In our home you have created for me a microcosm of serenity, security, and love. When we are together at home, isolated from the outside world, I feel a great sense of peace and tranquility.

40. Liveability Quotient
You have elevated my liveability quotient, heightened my personal standards of romance, devotion, gratification, and feelings of love.

41. Cosmic Breath
Together we create a wealth of positive energy, and that energy is released and flows freely into the atmosphere, enhancing the cosmos.

42. Feelings Magnified
I love you deeply, and know within my heart that that feeling is magnified each and every day, and it grows exponentially with each touch, each kiss, and each caress.

43. Culmination
You are the love of my life and the purpose of my existence. You are the culmination of all my reading, my life's lessons, and the radiant consequence of all my choices.

44. Extreme Love

I adore you. You have infused my life with harmony and extreme love. Thank you for every precious kiss, every hug, every thought and every act of love. You are the love of my life.

45. Gratitude

I am so grateful that we found one another and recognized immediately the surge of love that we generated within each other.

46. Common Thread

The common thread of our life is the love that we share and the awesome sense of renewal we each experience on returning home to one another's arms at the end of each day.

47. Inner Space

The complexities of the world are left at our threshold as we enter our inner space, simplify our lives, and join together to nourish our love and amplify our romance.

48. Rituals of Our Life
You are the keeper of the rituals of our life, the guardian of our stability and the maintainer of our sharp focus.

49. Life Garden
The seeds of integrity, honesty, respect, honor, and purity will be nourished by our daily rituals, and blossoms will be scattered throughout our days and nights to form a magnificent life garden.

50. Beacon
When I am away from home, you serve as a beacon guiding me back to our love nest. The beacon is atop a lighthouse that represents security, foundation, and honesty. That lighthouse is our relationship and our mutual love.

51. Magical Fullness
You fill my life with magical experiences, making each day a wondrous dream-come-true.

52. Illuminating Pleasures

You converted my fantasies into tangible days and nights of intimate and illuminating pleasure.

53. Clarity

In my mental self-exploration, clarity emerges, revealing my deep love for you and all that you mean to me.

54. Seasons

It is said that everything has a season. If that is true, this is our season. This is our time for loving, for companionship, for togetherness, for romance, for communication, for fun, and for happiness.

55. Evolution

You are quieting my soul, bringing it into balance, and influencing its evolution toward perfection.

56. Miracle
Our relationship is like a miracle which is self-renewing, and keeps blossoming and unfolding into a beautiful life adventure.

57. In Sync
We are so in sync on every level that our souls and mindsets have meshed together beautifully, and we are one. We have become one, and our union is almost seamless.

58. My Sun, Moon, and Stars
You are my sun and you light my life with perpetual sunshine and warm rays of love and happiness. You are also my moon and stars and you fill my evenings with passion and ecstasy.

59. New Beginnings
Spring is a time of rebirth and new beginnings. Our love is providing a continual nourishing shower which causes the seeds of our relationship to grow and blossom into a beautiful, strong, healthy, and lifelong union.

60. Music and Rhythms of Our Life
I love the music and rhythms of our life. I treasure the sound of your breathing next to me in bed, and the sound of your voice encouraging me in the morning, and the songs we dance to in the evening, and the music we make love to at night.

61. Compass
You are my light and my compass. You keep me centered and give me direction. You are my shining star. I love you with all my heart.

62. Love Connection
Our meeting in that cubic centimeter of chance and millisecond of time was a miracle in itself. Miraculously by a few strokes of the keyboard, we introduced ourselves. How very quickly that electronic connection turned into a deep love connection with mutual respect for one another, that will last a lifetime.

63. Vision
You are my idea of the perfect partner. Together we will create our own vision, and walk hand in hand into the future to achieve that vision.

64. Life is a Journey
There is a saying: *Life is a journey. Waltz, don't walk* Our life together is a beautiful journey, and we are waltzing through it together.

65. Positive Energy
Loving you fills me with a continual flow of positive energy, making me better at everything I do and giving me a positive, happy outlook.

66. Celebrating Us
We celebrate *us*, our love, and our beautiful relationship because our minds, bodies, and spirits are truly on the same wavelength and are completely in sync.

67. Magnify
Together we will do great things, and our love will continue to magnify and become more powerful as time goes by.

68. Exhilarating Adventure
We have embarked on an exhilarating adventure into our future together. You make every day of that adventure wonderful and extraordinary.

69. As Long as We're Together
Whether we are at home together or traveling to exotic places, as long as we are together, all is right with our world.

70. Love of My Life
In you, I have found the love of my life, and I delight in loving you intensely and completely.

71. You've Got Mail!
A highlight of my day is checking my e-mail, hearing "You've Got Mail!" and finding another beautiful, priceless e-mail message from you. I love the metaphors and beautiful images you weave into your messages.

72. Mosaic of Memories
We are creating a mosaic of life together. Each day we add more colorful designs to that beautiful mosaic as we insert more memory tiles of brilliant hues into those designs that are uniquely ours

73. Success is So Much Sweeter
Success is so much sweeter with you to share it with, and our visions seem much more reachable with us working together.

74. Energized By Your Love
Loving you makes every day a special and positive experience and helps me to stay centered.

75. Remembering What's Important
On days that seem to have life's little annoyances, these annoyances begin to fade away and I realize that everything important is wonderful in my life and that I have everything I ever wanted in you, my darling.

76. Incandescent

You are fabulous! You turn on my internal engine and cause it to ignite with the heat of your passion, giving me an inner glow radiating so that everyone notices the radiance.

77. My Rock, My Inspiration

You are my rock, my inspiration, my heart of hearts, and love of my life.

78. Tremendous Growth

Ever since we met, I have experienced tremendous growth of my emotional bank account, not only from the deposits received in your wonderful, loving messages, but also from the deposits I've given to your emotional bank account.

79. The Road that Has Made All the Difference

Our lives took us on a journey where we took the road less traveled by—the cyberpathway which led to our meeting, and that has definitely made all the difference. Our life couldn't be better.

80. Kindred Spirits
You and I are kindred spirits and our individual compasses have the same markings and the needles pointing to the same direction.

81. Vitality
You breathe vitality and enthusiasm into our love and into our marriage, and the energy I receive from you moves me to a higher vibration.

82. Catalyst
You are the catalyst that is helping me to grow and to expand my perspective on life. You help me grow emotionally, intellectually, and spiritually.

83. Diamond
Our love is like the facets of a sparkling diamond, each facet reflecting the light differently and the brilliance of all the facets combined illuminating our days with sunshine and true happiness.

84. Awakened
You have awakened within me the deepest and truest love which I share with you because you love me so completely and intensely.

85. Fabulous
Our love is truly fabulous, and I feel extremely rich and fortunate to be blessed with your incredible love.

86. Whispered Encouragement
Sometimes the message of love is delivered as whispered encouragement, or during a telephone call, often in writing, and most frequently in the midst of a warm and tender hug.

87. Cosmic Proportions
The discovery of our true love is a spectacular sensation whose magnitude reaches cosmic proportions in my heart.

88. Reflection

Last night I had a conversation with my reflection in the mirror. My image and I talked about the steps we took to alter our patterns of living and our need to meet someone wonderful to share our future with. Then you and I met, and my mirrored-image had a companion to share in the mirror.

89. Multi-sensory

I love that we can perceive the world from the multi-sensory level and share our feelings, insights, and thoughts so comfortably. You create and excite tremendous multi-sensory stimuli in me.

90. Metaphysical

You are awesome! You heighten my senses and bring so much sunshine to me. You are such a delight to me and I love loving you, and love the way that you love me.

91. Rejuvenated

You have truly rejuvenated my life with your powerful love. Your e-mail messages, little notes, phone calls, words of affirmations, and your loving touch all rejuvenate my body, my spirit, and my mind every minute of each day.

92. Priceless Gifts

You have given me so many priceless gifts of beautiful messages with wonderful, loving thoughts exquisitely expressed, numerous acts of kindness and service, and an abundance of deep, passionate, and sincere love. These are things that I will always have and will always treasure. They are symbols and constant reminders of your love for me and of my love for you.

93. Gifts Wrapped in Love

Each new day is a gift that comes wrapped in love.

94. Magic, Marvel, and Mystery

Our love is filled with magic, wonder, and mystery. You make every day magical, and everything we do filled with wonder. *You* are the magic in my life.

95. Flow of Synchronicity

We seem to be surrounded by a flow of synchronicity and it has allowed us to experience many remarkable events that have enhanced our love.

96. Savor
Your touch and taste linger on my lips and heighten my excitement, imagination, and anticipation. You pleasure me so very much.

97. Wonderful Reward
You are the culmination of all my preparation for this chapter of my life and the wonderful reward for all my reading, learning, and life's choices.

98. Vacuum
You have filled the vacuum of my life magnificently and completely. You have helped me to reorganize my priorities and to appreciate the really important things in life.

99. Loving You
I adore you, and constantly count my blessings to be with you.

100. Life's Garden
I love our life garden that has blossomed and will continue to blossom from the seeds of mutual love that we have sown together.

101. Rooms of our Life
Of the many rooms in our home, the dining room has become the center of our expression, sharing of ideas and concepts. It is a room that serves as an eating area, a spiritual center, the gift-wrapping table, the area of candlelit elegance each evening, and the focal point of intense discussions on a wide variety of subjects. We plan there, we reminisce, we dine, we share, we kiss, we give thanks, we toast our love and our longevity. It is so much more than an eating place.

102. The Thin Line
There is a very thin line that represents the present time. It separates the rich heritage of our beautiful memories and the sweetest days that the future holds for us.

103 Splendor
It is no accident that we live a life of romantic splendor. You treat me with such exquisite love, and share your affections abundantly.

104. Clean Slates
You and I come together with clean slates. To me, you are innocent and pure, and our love is one of discovery of that innocence and purity

105. Joyful Simplicities
The joyful simplicities of our life are so meaningful and they bring me feelings of deep, deep gratitude.

106. Energizes
You've made my life so beautiful, contented, and fulfilled. Your love energizes me, fuels me to do more, to grow, and be a better person. I love you with all my heart.

107. Extraordinary Sense of Tranquility
You have created for me an extraordinary sense of peace, contentment, and tranquility within your arms.

108. Goals, Dreams, and Visions
I love traveling on the journey toward our goals, dreams, and visions hand in hand entwined with you.

109. Wondrous Realities
Together we are creating wondrous realities and future possibilities to share. I love our life's journey.

110. Togetherness
You delight and pleasure me so very much. Life with you is beautiful and glorious. I bless every day of our togetherness.

111. Transferred Energy
Our first physical contact transferred a significant burst of energy that exploded into true love. We were both receptive, willing and able, to share our individual auras with one another to create an even greater electrified space surrounding us.

112. Abundant Harvest of Gifts of Love
The abundant harvest of gifts of love that you bestow upon me are beyond my wildest dreams and imaginings.

113. Heartbeat
I love our life and the relationship that has developed and matured between us. You accelerate my heartbeat with your warm and loving touch.

114. Recesses of My Soul
When I introspect and examine the deepest recesses of my soul I am joyous that you have satisfied the constant craving within me for love.

115. Comfortable Cushion in My Life
You are as a comfortable cushion in my life, softening my surroundings, giving peace to my heart , and solace to my soul.

116. Consuming Passion
My life is now rich with the resonance of your love as you bestow your consuming passion upon me.

117. Tune of Contentment
I whistle tunes of contentment, hum melodies of mirth, and sing songs of satisfaction since first we met.

118. Pursuit of Happiness Scale
On the pursuit of happiness scale, you rate beyond the limits of the spectrum. You have made my life so fantastic.

119. Demystified
Together we have demystified the art of relationships and formed a pathway into our future that is aligned with happiness, contentment, and love.

120. Subatomic Happiness
You make me so happy, and please each and every subatomic particle that comprises the cells in my body.

121. Heartbeat Acceleration
You accelerate my heartbeat with your warm and loving touch.

122. Poetic Life
We live a poetic life that is filled with love, commitment and honor.

123. Passionate Pursuit
In my passionate pursuit of happiness you appeared, and I had to raise my expectations to match your level.

124. Gravitational Equilibrium
You have provided me with both gravitational and emotional equilibrium. Our personal patterns of living have melded together so remarkably.

125. Empowered

You have transformed me and empowered me to be the very best I have ever been in my life.

126. Touch of Your Skin

The touch of your skin, the warmth of your breath, the quickened beating of your heart all bring me to new heights of pleasure and anticipation

127. Affirmations of Love

You thrill my inner spirit when you speak affirmations of your love for me, and it is with a grateful heart that we each share one love.

128. Persistent Joyfulness

You thrill me with your love, your attention to my welfare, your persistent joyfulness, and your desire to be the best.

129. Rituals of Love
Our rituals of love symbolize the most important times of our lives, and they are enriching our souls.

130. Spirit of Our Journey
The spirit of our journey, the pursuit of our passions, and the overwhelming need to court our souls' contentment are fulfilled in our love.

131. Personal Passport
You have provided me with a personal passport to happiness. If you were to open my passport book, you would see all the pleasurable stops we have made so far on our trip through life. You are a magnificent traveling companion, and I love you so very much.

132. Balancing My Worlds
Having you to come home to each afternoon has brought balance to my outer and inner worlds. You are the love of my life and the most important treasure that I have, and I will always cherish you.

133. Creative Destiny
My creative destiny has found its home within our life together.

134. Enthralled
I was captivated by you, and willingly became enthralled with our future potential.

135. Vibrations
Minds, bodies, and souls each speak a different language and respond to varying vibrations of energy. Through the exchange of LovE-mails, we learned that our minds' languages resonated in unison.

136. Soul Rejoices
My soul rejoices and is gratified that the end of its search for a true soul-mate has been achieved.

137. True Essence

I may return to enjoy another life and to learn the true essence of myself. Yet, I want to savor the one I am living with you right now. You are a loving guide escorting my soul through the lessons it must learn in this life.

138. Doorway

I opened the doorway to the love compartment within my heart, and you filled all of the empty spaces with your love.

139. Perfection

My soul knows what needs to advance to the next level toward perfection, and that is why it chose you for me.

140. Priceless Gift

You are a priceless gift that I have been entrusted to hold and care for, and I shall do so with great tenderness and honor.

141. Restorative Gift
You have salvaged my life and handed it back to me as a restorative gift, wrapped in the bright glow of your love and tied with a bow of encouragement.

142. Prime Time
When we are together, we enjoy the hush of harmony, the warmth of being nurtured, the dedication to each other, and the expression of our mutual love.

143. Sacred Continuum
In the sacred continuum of life, you have given me tender refuge, and fed my hungry heart with your love.

144. Biological Urges
My biological urges and instincts are immediately satisfied by your presence and appeased by our love.

145. Web of My Life
In the web of my life, you have woven a strand that supports the entire fabric of my existence. Thank you, my darling.

146. Prince Among Men
You are a prince among men, and I adore you. You make me feel so loved and cherished, and you cause my soul to soar higher and my heart to dance with joy every day.

147. Charmed Life
What a charmed and wonderful life we live. Since first we met, being together has been magnificent, beautiful, and loving.

148. Deposits in Our Treasury of Memories
We are continually creating exquisitely beautiful deposits in our treasury of memories for us to reminisce about and savor for years to come.

149. Smile and Glow

You make me so very, very happy, and cause me to smile and glow radiantly with delight, joy, and contentment all the time. You are a precious gift, and I treasure you.

150. Unbelievably Happy

You and I will take perennial pleasure in the adventures and fulfillment that we will share together. You make me unbelievably happy.

151. Light Years

You are truly the light and love of my life. Your light shines into my soul and illuminates my heart and mind, as well as my spirit. I adore you, sweetheart, and look forward to many "light years" with you.

152. Never in My Life

Never in my life have I felt so in tune with anyone as I do with you.

153. Life's Lessons

I have learned so much from you about love and about other life's lessons, and you have caused me to grow and become a better and more complete person. Thank you for making our life so fantastic and so bright and uplifting.

154. Seamlessly Connected

You and I are seamlessly connected, and our intimate bond grows stronger and stronger with each passing day.

155. Appreciate Our Love

Our love has grown and blossomed and become deeper with each day. We live a charmed, wonderful life, and take time to celebrate and appreciate our love and our togetherness.

156. Perfect Match

We are fabulous together and are a perfect match. I love loving you and I love the way you love me.

157. Adore You

You are a precious gift, and I treasure you. I adore you, my darling, and always will. I love you so very much and thank you for loving me as intensely as you do.

158. Ecstatic

Thank you for making me so unbelievably happy and contented. You cause me to smile on the outside, glow with joy on the inside, and feel completely ecstatic and fulfilled.

159. Rainy Days

Even on a rainy day, you bathe me with rays of sunshine that appear to radiate from you. You are so positive and have such light and good energy. I adore you, and will love you forever.

160. Priorities

From the moment we came together, we have shared the same priorities in our lives. You are my highest priority and I am yours.

161. Lengthy Journey

As we travel on our hopefully, very lengthy journey through life together, each of us sheds light into the other's soul and heart. The result is a combined light that is much more brilliant and radiant than the light of our two souls.

162. Knight in Shining Armor

Thank you for being my knight in shining armor. You are valiant and wonderful.

I adore you, my darling.

163. Powerful Pull

Each time we are separated, I feel a powerful, pleasurable pull toward you.

I love the wondrous ways we live and love together.

164. Changing Seasons

As the seasons change from the warmth of the summer's mornings to the coolness of autumn, I cannot help but reflect on the magnificent changes that have taken place in my life since first we met.

165. Transformation
Your love has transformed my energies to satisfy my deepest yearnings. The sharing of one love and the profound intimacy that we have discovered has made our union filled with intense pleasure and significance.

166. Aura
Our relationship is a spiritual experience that, to this time in my life, has been unknown. You refresh my spirit with your warming aura, and your soothing aroma causes me to continually pause to count my many blessings.

167. We are One
You are so beautiful, and I love that you take pride in your appearance and in your health. We are certainly one when it comes to our priorities in life. You are awesome. I treasure each and every day together.

168. Significant
What significant things have I done to deserve you as a reward? As we live our daily lives, we are evidently accumulating points, and when we have accumulated the required amount, then wonderful things begin to happen.

169. Burst of Energy
Our first physical contact resulted in a powerful burst of energy that exploded into a deep, true love. Our hearts, minds, and souls merged and created an even greater energy field surrounding us.

170. Between Heaven and Earth
You are my link between heaven and earth, and have created a paradise for me within your loving arms.

171. Messages of Love
Your messages are so wonderful, and make me feel so loved and cherished. We are so in tune with one another and match in every aspect of our being. Our love is for today and for all our tomorrows. It will be magnificent and everlasting.

172. Beyond My Dreams
The abundance of gifts and acts of love that you bestow upon me are greater than my dreams could imagine. My love for you is constant, and grows stronger and deeper in magnitude each day.

173. Being Together
What a charmed and wonderful life we live. The first year of our being together has been magnificent, beautiful and loving. I look forward to many, many years together celebrating our love and our union, and doing good things together.

174. Shining Brightly
Our love is a light for everyone around us. We will continue to keep that light shining brightly and filled with love forever.

175. Top Priority
You are my life's top priority. I treasure you and our time together. Our life is radiant and beautiful, and filled with magic, love, and promise. I love the simple things that we do everyday to make our life wonderful and happy, and to honor one another.

176. ABC's of Love

I LOVE YOU ARDENTLY AND AFFECTIONATELY,
I LOVE YOU BOLDLY AND BEAUTIFULLY,
I LOVE YOU COMPLETELY AND CONFIDENTLY,
I LOVE YOU DEEPLY AND DELIBERATELY
I LOVE YOU EAGERLY AND ECSTATICALLY,
I LOVE YOU FEVERISHLY AND FULLY,
I LOVE YOU GENUINELY AND GRACIOUSLY,
I LOVE YOU HAPPILY AND HEARTILY,
I LOVE YOU INTIMATELY AND IMPORTANTLY,
I LOVE YOU JOYOUSLY AND JEALOUSLY,
I LOVE YOU KINDLY AND KNOWLEDGEABLY,
I LOVE YOU LOVINGLY AND LUSCIOUSLY,
I LOVE YOU MIGHTILY AND MARVELOUSLY,
I LOVE YOU NURTURINGLY AND NICELY,
I LOVE YOU OPENLY AND OBVIOUSLY,
I LOVE YOU PROUDLY AND PURPOSEFULLY,
I LOVE YOU QUIETLY AND QUANTUMLY,
I LOVE YOU REVERENTLY AND ROMANTICALLY,
I LOVE YOU SOLEMNLY AND STRONGLY,
I LOVE YOU TENDERLY AND TENACIOUSLY,
I LOVE YOU UNDENIABLY AND UNBEATABLY,
I LOVE YOU VIGOROUSLY AND VALUABLY,
I LOVE YOU WARMLY AND WONDERFULLY,
I LOVE YOU ZESTFULLY AND ZEALOUSLY.

177. History

Our past history has been amazingly wonderful. You are a rare find. I love being with you and sharing the mundane and the magnificent together.

178. Unknowingly

You are the love of my life, and the one I have been unknowingly preparing for all these years. Together we are making a beautiful future. A future filled with delight, ecstasy, meaning, strengthening of spirit, true love and joy.

179. Bond Everlasting

You are my source of happiness. Our bond is everlasting. You have brought me into a state of bliss that surmounts anything I have experienced or imagined in my entire life. I love you completely and deeply.

180. Appreciating You

I constantly pause throughout the day and evening to be thankful and appreciative of the magnificent treasure that you are. You make our life wonderful and beautiful every single day.

181. Things that Please Us Immensely

I love the simple things that we do every day to make our life wonderful and to honor one another. Sharing breakfast, sending one another beautiful LovE-mail messages, dining and dancing by candlelight, watching movies and reading together, making love and falling asleep in one another's arms are some of the things that please us immensely and cause our life to be enchanting and magnificent.

182. Shining Star

You are my shining star, my inspiration, my encourager, lover, soul mate, and best friend. I would not be who I am without your influence. You cause me to grow and become a better person.

183. Homecoming

You are the love of my life and I treasure you. When you return home each day, my heart leaps with excitement and delight.

184. Captivated

From the start, I was captivated by you, and very quickly fell in love with you. You magnetically attracted me to you, and won over my heart, mind, and spirit.

185. Wishing on Billions of Stars

I love to sit on our balcony with you and view the stars and constellations. If I could wish upon all of the billions and billions of stars in the universe, I would wish for us to have a very long life to enjoy the magnificent love and fantastic relationship that we have created and now share.

186. North Star

You are my North Star, and I can set my course toward a better life of love and goodness with you. You exude star-shine, causing me to glow and emanate light for others.

187. Dreams Come True

You are making all of my dreams come true, and together we are planning our goals and visions for the future, and making those come true.

188. Storybook Romance

I dreamed about a perfect relationship, and thought it was unattainable. Then you came into my life, and every day has been like a fairy tale or storybook romance.

189. Sweet Love
You are my wonderful, handsome, sweet love of my life. I want to make you the happiest husband on earth. I want to please you always and be the best wife possible to you. I love you with all my heart, and will love you forever.

190. Intellectual Love
You are so good for me. You make me feel protected, loved, sexy, beautiful, cherished, and valued. I adore you, and love the person that you are. You are a beautiful human being and an awesome lover. You are definitely my soul-mate and intellectual love, as well as romantic love.

191. Swept Off My Feet
I met a prince who swept me off my feet, captured my heart, and made my dreams all come true. You have made me feel like a princess, and I am the happiest woman in the world.

192. Dancing on the Balcony
Life with you is a continual, beautiful adventure. We are beginning to build a bank of wonderful experiences that are uniquely ours. Dancing on the balcony under the moon and the stars with you is one of those beautiful memories I will always treasure.

193. Missing You

I feel an empty space when we are separated, even though I know that it is only temporary, and we will soon be rejoined. You absolutely delight all my senses and bring me to new heights of passion. You expand my heart, allowing more of your love to enter and reside in my heart permanently.

194. Deliciously Wonderful

I love you more than chocolate, and more than anything in the world. You are my dream husband, and life with you is deliciously wonderful and so filled with promise. I will savor our love always.

195. Into Every Prayer

When we talked, when we met, when we kissed, and when we made love, you immediately fit into every prayer, every dream, every visualization, and every image of the ideal. Perfection is your name.

196. Watching You

Watching you interact with others has made me see why I love you so deeply. You are so warm, caring, and positive. Everyone who comes into contact with you leaves a happier person. You are a warm, magnificent human being, and I love you intensely and completely.

197. Hyper-time

Our love became like the films we have seen where the opening of a beautiful flower is speeded up, and, in seconds, we see what it takes days to accomplish. Our love blossomed in hours into a relationship that has taken years to mature in others. During that hyper-time, and to this very minute, I have never doubted or questioned my decision to love you and to walk hand in hand together into the future.

198. Soul Skills

Up until the time we met, we had each developed our people skills by reading, learning, teaching, discussing, experimenting, and implementing. When we met, we incorporated all of those skills into "soul skills" that allow us to share each other at the highest plane of love and intimacy.

199. Overdrive

We transcended the everyday acts of getting to know one another because we knew ourselves. Understanding our own wants and needs allowed us to put our love into overdrive, and know from the very beginning that we had found our soul-mates.

200. Interwoven
Our lives are entwined into a beautiful, colorful, dynamic tapestry of life. The combination of the two of us makes the pattern of the tapestry exquisite and beautiful. Our lives are interwoven with such deep love and commitment that our union will last forever.

201. Twilight
As we experience the waning sun return to the other side of the world and marvel at the brilliance of colors in the cloud formations, I cannot help but appreciate the emotional warmth that you have brought into my life.

202. Glimmering Lights, Flickering Candles
As the lights of the night glimmer and the flame of the candles flicker, we burn with emotion and express those feelings in our lovemaking. My love for you echoes within me and creates a deep longing for our togetherness.

203. Creative Conduit
You have allowed me to be the person I was intended to be. You make me happier than I have ever been in my life. You have nurtured a creative conduit in the form of my writing these LovEmail messages to you.

204. Sunrise

Thank you for being so magnificent and wonderful. Each day you bathe me with rays of sunshine and love. My sun rises with you. You give me warmth, light, hope and promise for each day just as each sunrise does.

205. Reaching Higher Peaks

Your enthusiasm, support, and love have energized me and helped me to reach higher peaks. There hasn't been a single day since we first met that has not been a really good day.

206. Big Star

I want you to know that you are a Big Star in my book. You are an awesome husband, lover, and partner. You are brilliant and fantastic in every way. Your presence and participation have enhanced everything I do.

207. Most Important Person in My World

You inspire me, motivate me to soar, and accomplish more. We work so well together and we play so beautifully together. You are my hero and my ideal. You are the shining light in my life, and the most important person in my world.

208. Beautiful Dream

Last night, as we danced by candlelight in the kitchen, I felt as though I was having a beautiful dream and woke to find it was real. I was dancing with my prince in a candlelight ballroom in our own castle. You are my prince. You are magnificent and handsome, sexy and loving, brilliant and fun. I adore you.

209. Sense of Accomplishment

I have enjoyed the smell of success along my path, but the true and deep sense of accomplishment always remained elusive. You have changed the course of my life and pointed me in the direction of self-actualization.

210. Augmenting my Inner Creative Voice

With your guidance, I have been able to enjoy and harmonize my expanded sense of creativity and the effects of the enormous love that we share. Your encouragement has brought to the surface a higher harmonic, adding to and augmenting my inner creative voice.

211. Unit of ONE
We complement and support each other with such love, harmony, and enthusiasm. The unit of ONE that we have become is stronger and more magnificent than the two of us individually.

212. Propel Me to New Heights
Your enthusiasm and support help propel me to new heights. My mission in life is to give you that same level of support and enthusiasm, and make you feel self-actualized, loved, and treasured. You are the most important person in my world, and I love you with all my heart.

213. Private Moments
I honor our relationship. Our intimate love is a fantastic experience. You make me feel so beautiful and fulfilled, and I know that those feelings are shared. We will renew our vows of love and re-experience those private moments that are so meaningful to us both. Our lives will meld into one wonderful existence.

214. Getting Closer

I surrender myself to you completely. Our relationship is so magnificent. We are absolutely made to be with each other. I love you dearly, and think about you constantly. I think about what a wonderful life we are having and are going to have, day by day, week by week, month by month, and year by year.

215. Replenishing the Feelings of Love

The image of the twilight and the sinking sun bringing on the hushed silence of night, replenishes the deep feelings of love that I have for you.

As the light and warmth disappear outdoors, our light and warmth are just beginning to express themselves indoors.

216. Golden Sunbeams of Love

Being in your strong arms and looking up into your handsome face, gives me such a sense of security and love. My sun rises each time I see your beautiful, warm smile and feel the warmth you exude. You bathe me in golden sunbeams of love.

217. Bow of Promise

You are a wonderful gift that has been bestowed upon me. You came wrapped in love and tied with a bow of promise for a beautiful future.

218. Romantic Setting

I love the amorous side of you and that you take time to create a perfect romantic setting, with candles, soft music, flowers, the moon and stars as a canopy, and love notes left on my desk and around the house.

219. Reading Together

I love reading together, and hope that it is an exercise that we always continue, whether it be our emails, books, magazines, or cereal boxes. Just sitting and being near you and sharing our time together is delightful.

220. Blue Angels

We are the Blue Angels or synchronized swimmers in the way that we think, act, and fit together. We have established an inseparable bond and union that unites us and forms us into a single body, mind, and spirit.

221. Swing and Sway
Like couples ice skating, we swing and sway together to life's music, each doing our own pirouetting, and yet rejoining for the majority of the dance.

222. Fabric
I love you dearly, and you have become a part of me as if we had been sewn together within the same fabric. Together we make a beautiful tapestry of love, for one another. I treasure you and pray that I can always be the man you can treasure in return.

223. Serenity
You have helped me to live and develop both outwardly and inwardly. Outwardly in the love that is written all over my face, for all the world to see as we walk hand in hand. Inwardly, in the serenity I experience when we are together and the passionate feelings I have for you. You have made our love a deeply spiritual love that stabilizes the delicate balance of living.

224. Past, Present, Future

I have a deep appreciation for my past because it prepared me for our relationship. I have an enriched sense of the present because of the love we share. And, I have a joyous anticipation of the future because of the harmonious life we live.

225. Turned My Darkness Into Light

You have turned my darkness into light . My entire world and future changed miraculously when we first met and when you agreed to be my wife. I will forever rejoice at our union.

226. From the Height of the Mountains

From the height of the mountains to the depth of the deserts, my love for you is deep and sincere. As the oceans are far below the surface of the land, my love for you is elevated above the surface of all other loves. I am so thankful that you are mine and return my love

227. Infusion of Love
You are vital to my peace of mind and sense of well-being. Each time we come together, I re-acquaint myself with your power, energy, and your life-enhancing infusion of love into my life. Thank you, my darling, my love, my wife.

228. Creative Energy
The creative energy that you possess, the warmth of your touch, your smiling face, and your marvelous sense of humor all form an aura around the chairs, the pictures, the books, and all the other items that comprise the anatomy of our home.

229. Breathless
Just talking about you gives me such a thrill, and thinking my private thoughts about you makes me excited and breathless.

230. Nourishing My Soul
You are nourishing my soul and helping it evolve to higher levels. Together we will achieve new heights, and when we are together, anything is possible.

231. Facing Life's Joys and Challenges
We will face life's joys and challenges together, and our love will become stronger and more enriched as a result.

232. Direction of My Existence
You have illuminated my life and changed the entire direction of my existence.

233. Unlimited Joy
We will have unlimited joy, peace, and harmony. You are my source for happiness. Our bond is everlasting.

234. Intimacies
You are beautiful, and our intimacies give me great joy. Our loving secrets give the promise of marvelous possibilities for years and years to come.

235. Tomorrows
You are my treasure, and I treasure our love, our loving, our future, and all of our tomorrows.

236. Ever Aware
I want you to be ever-aware of my presence, whether together or apart, and the knowledge that I am with you in my thoughts, and we are together in our goals and dreams.

237. Melted My Heart
You delight my entire being. You have melted my heart and captivated my soul. You are fabulous, and I treasure you and our relationship.

238. Reverence
It is with deep reverence that I write these words, "I LOVE YOU." The repetition of these words in our conversations and our affirmations should not diminish their meaning and the sincerity with which they are spoken.

239. Beginnings
The first time we met was the beginning of great transformations in my life. The changes have caused a renewal of my spirit and joy to my world.

240. Accomplishment
You have changed my pattern of energy to a higher level of vibration. You set me on a path of accomplishment and joy.

241. Cast New Light
You have released my existence from its chains and set it free and into motion with the joyousness that was truly mine to have. You have softened my soul and cast new light into it.

242. Special Alignment
We are in a special alignment that makes us both so happy and fulfilled. Our flow of life is smooth and sweet and I am loving it. You are my every wish come true.

243. Forces That Brought Us Together
I celebrate our marriage and our love every day and every night in my heart, and thank whatever forces brought us together.

244. Helping Me Grow
You are the catalyst in my life helping me grow emotionally, intellectually, and spiritually.

245. Complement Each Other
I love our life, and love that we challenge and complement each other toward greater insights of ourselves and of the world around us.

246. Spring In My Step
You bring out the shine in life and the spring in my step. I cherish you and our life together. I love the glow and energy that you bring to our marriage.

247. Intuition

Through glimmers of intuition, a revelation materializes of our wonderful life together and the future our togetherness will bring.

248. Secure With You

Secure with you and me together, our home gives me a great deal of appreciation for our love and the precious gifts we share.

249. Dearly and Deeply

You have endowed me with love. I love you dearly and deeply and will always be there for you.

250. Essential Energy

As the essential energy of our love is allowed to rise, the cosmic breath of love's renewal continually envelopes us with its presence.

251. Generated By Love
Our love is generated and regenerated by our touch, our lovemaking, our sense of honor for one another, and the respect we have for our relationship.

252. DNA
You and I are so perfect together. Our DNA might be very different, but our love, our dreams, our visions, our goals, our needs, and our pathways are superimposed and aligned.

253. Exploration
It did not take a lot of inner exploration to determine that I had found a treasure that could transform my dreams into reality.

254. Tranquility
You and I have found love, peace, order, and tranquility within our interior doors. I love you deeply and treasure our life together. Thank you for bringing contentment to my life.

255. Fertile Ground
In the fertile ground of our life, we have sown the seeds of mutual love—a love that is real for today and will blossom into the dreams of our tomorrows.

256. Multidimensional Splendor
We are living in multidimensional splendor, enjoying each other at so many different levels.

257. Future Full of Possibilities
You have created a future full of possibilities that we will share together.

258. Manifestation of My Visualizations
You are my dream come true, and the manifestation of my visualizations. I love you very much.

259. Overwhelming Happiness
Your love has changed the course and direction of my life, and has contributed to my overwhelming happiness and joy.

260. By Love Am I Possessed
By love am I possessed, and you are the object of that profound emotion.

261. Time We Have Together
I treasure you and this time we have together. May our time be long and as fulfilling as our past years have been.

262. Pure Joyousness
You have made me feel alive again, and have enabled me to experience pure joyousness. I thank God or whatever forces brought us together.

263. Matched Perfectly

We match perfectly on every level—romantically, intellectually, emotionally, mentally, spiritually. We have the same priorities, both emphasize the positive, and value a sense of humor.

264. Better Together

Together we are much better than we are as two separate persons. Our union has strengthened and enhanced us as individuals.

265. Given My Life Purpose

You have given my life purpose and unbelievable happiness and contentment.

266. Flowering Experiences

We are growing a beautiful garden of flowering experiences and memories that are ours alone.

267. Glow and Smile
These rhythms of our life make me glow and smile constantly, and make me feel like dancing through each day. You are magnificent and I adore you.

268. Journey Will Always Be Magical
I love dancing through life and traveling on life's journey with you. I pray that our journey will always be as magical and wondrous as it is now.

269. Brightened My Life
You've brightened my life so much that even on cloudy or rainy days, I have my own inner supply of sunshine derived from your love and devotion.

270. Greatest Delight
Loving you is the greatest delight and pleasure of my life.

271. Enjoying The Journey
Our goals, our vision, our values, and priorities have steered us both onto the same pathway. Now we are sharing and enjoying the journey together toward our shared vision.

272. Powerful Together
We are so powerful together. We work together so beautifully on so many levels, whether a private level or a public level, striving to make the world a better place.

273. Love Notes
You make every day of my life wondrous and happy with all of the special things that you do for me. I love finding your beautiful love notes on the bathroom counter or in my email. I delight in finding a bouquet of flowers in the refrigerator. I love our romantic, candlelight dinners, and I love dancing all through the house with you. l love our life.

274. Beautiful Life Together
Being with you is a gift in itself, and I treasure our beautiful life together.

275. Potential of Achievement

Our love has blossomed and grown into a magnificent powerful energy that will continue to fuel us to do great things together. We haven't even come close to our full potential of achievement.

276. Discovering

We are going to have a wonderful life discovering our potential and doing good things together. I love loving you and being loved by you.

277. Hidden Treasures

Your beautiful LovEmail messages are like little hidden treasures, gift-wrapped with so much love, in beautiful sparkling, exquisite little golden boxes waiting for me to open them.

278. Unwrapping Each One

I love discovering your beautiful love messages that are like hidden treasures, waiting to be carefully unwrapped. I experience a thrill as I read them over and over again.

279. Experiences
Our beautiful life's experiences are like colorful tiles comprising our exquisite mosaic of life.

280. Exclusively Ours
We are creating a Mosaic of Memories that will be exclusively ours forever and will continue to grow and become more and more beautiful with time.

281. Ordinary to Marvelous
You have transformed my life from the ordinary to the marvelous.

282. Happen Together
You have made all of our accomplishments more joyous and exciting because we are making them happen together.

283. Unconditional Love

Thank you for everything you do for me and for loving me as unconditionally and as completely as you do. I love you deeply, completely, and unconditionally, and I love loving you.

284. Thrill Every Cell

You thrill every cell in my body and excite and stimulate me beyond belief.

285. Uniquely Special

I love our life and the many uniquely special things we do to please one another in so many exciting ways.

286. Share Ideas

We share ideas for our present and future and then act to make our dreams become realities.

287. Integrity to My Life
You give meaning and integrity to my life, and give unconditional love and deep commitment to me. I love you deeply and completely and will always treasure you.

288. Lives Touched
Since our lives touched, we have been enjoying growth emotionally, as well as spiritually, mentally, and in every way possible.

289. Cherish Every Minute
Our love, our relationship, our marriage, and our life are all magical and wonderful. I love our life together and cherish every minute with you.

290. Going Down the Path Hand in Hand
We are on the same path, and I love that we are going down that path hand in hand, loving one another so completely and intensely.

291. Focus Your Love
I love the way you love me and focus your love and energy on me and demonstrate that love with everything you do or say.

292. Incredible Happiness
You cause me to feel such incredible happiness and contentment that I actually feel energy inside me. I feel as though I am exuding energy in return to you all the time.

293. Challenge and Complement
I love our life and I love the way that we challenge and complement each other to develop greater insights of ourselves and of the universe.

294. Attraction
We have such a powerful attraction for each other, and bring each other such total contentment when we are together.

295. Every Choice Has a Future
Every choice has a future, and our choice to spend the rest of our lives together is moving us toward a beautiful future that is unfolding day by day.

296. Being Told that I am Loved
I begin each morning and end each day being told that I am loved. How marvelous a feeling, knowing that the someone I love, cherish, and adore returns those feelings to me throughout the day.

297. Bathed By Sensations
I am bathed by sensations of acceptance and approval. I need not reinvent myself to please someone else.

298. Knowledge of Your Love
My spiritual DNA delights with the knowledge that your love is not imaginary, but a real power of consciousness. I love you dearly and deeply, and experience your emotions as they are sent to me from your heart.

299. Joy to My Reflection
You have brought great joy to both me and my reflection, as we each now have someone to love on both sides of the mirror.

300. Image In The Mirror
When our image is not in the mirror, the mirror knows that when we return, our images will be smiling with the joy and happiness we share together.

301. I Love Looking At You
I love looking at you, and am thrilled by your touch, your smell, your taste and your voice.

302. The Completeness of Our Love
The completeness of our love makes our relationship permanent, magical, exciting fulfilling, and very special.

303. Fuels Me

You give me a tremendous supply of positive energy and that fuels me and helps me to be the very best I can be.

304. Outer Package

I love the inner person that you are and I love the outer package that you share so lovingly with me.

305. Life Together is Wonderful

Our life together is wonderful, magical, beautiful and loving.

306. Each New Day

Each new day is better and more wonderful than the day before because we make it happen.

307. Attuned to One Another

We are so attuned to one another's needs and desires, and we take time and effort each day to cherish one another.

308. Blessed
Ours is a union that is blessed.

309. Filled With Surprises
Our relationship is so magical and filled with wonderful surprises.

310. Ignites My Imagination
Life with you ignites my imagination, lights up my soul, and fires up my heart.

311. Becomes More Wonderful
Our relationship is fabulous, and becomes more wonderful as we find more ways to enhance our love and fulfill our dreams.

312. Imagination
Our imagination helps us to create a love and life for ourselves that far exceeds our dreams or our realities.

313. Master of My Being
You are the love of my life, the master of my being, the guardian of my contentment, and the joy of all my tomorrows.

314. Your Love Elevates Me
Your love elevates me to a state of complete bliss and joy, and I feel such powerful and infinite love for you.

315. Excitement to My Mind
You bring joy to my heart, excitement to my mind, and exhilaration to my soul.

316. Mission Is To Please
My mission is to please you completely and bring you to a state of elation and complete joy. I will love, honor, and treasure you always.

317. Before You Came Into My Life
Before you came into my life, everything was preparation for our meeting and union, and for the many years we have ahead to share.

318. Exude Happiness
You exude happiness, love, peace, and joy into my life. I will always love you with all my heart.

319. Connected Electronically
Ever since we connected electronically, we have been connecting on every level, emotionally, intellectually, psychologically, sexually, mentally, and spiritually.

320. Glorious Chapter of My Life
You have made this the most glorious chapter of my life, and have made me so fulfilled and excited about life and about our love.

321. Growth and Fulfillment
Our life together is so wonderful and I always feel that each day with you is one of growth, fulfillment, and happiness.

322. Honored My Life
You have honored my life and made it so much better by your presence.

323. Cells Burst With Joy
You make my cells burst with joy and my heart dance with love and excitement. I love loving you.

324. Seeds of Integrity
The seeds of integrity, honesty, respect, honor, and purity will continue to be cultivated and nourished by our daily rituals and by our love for one another.

325. Identity
Our life-garden will reflect our unique combined identity and needs and our mutual vision.

326. Sunshine of Good Times
With the sunshine of good times and the positive, good energy of our love and respect for one another, our life-garden will blossom into lives of meaning and significance together.

327. Home a Heaven on Earth
You have made our home a heaven on earth, and I thank you for the comfort and joy you have brought into my life as a result.

328. Fleeting Moment
Our present is but a fleeting moment that divides the past from the future. This makes it all the more important to enjoy and cherish each day as we do.

329. Every Minute of the Day
We regard each day as a gift and cherish one another every minute of the day.

330. Delicious Memories
By creating a treasury of beautiful days, we are making a rich bank of wonderful, delicious memories for us to recall and savor for years to come.

331. Comfort in My Heart
You have created such wonderful comfort in my heart and soul.

332. Centers of Emotion
You have caused my soul to heal, and you delight the centers of emotions within me.

333. Compassion
We will find within ourselves and within each other the compassion, courage, and wisdom to build a wonderful life and create a future that is beautiful, fulfilling, and meaningful.

334. Temporal to Triumphant
You have changed my life from temporal to triumphant.

335. Feast for My Eyes
You are a feast for my eyes. I love your size, your look, and your smell. You bring me to the essences of paradise with your sweet scents.

336. Warmth of You
I feel the warmth of you seeping into my body and raising my pleasure-level to new heights.

337. Hugs and Caresses
Your hugs and caresses sustain me and nourish my heart, and your kisses and affirmations stimulate and excite me.

338. So Loving
Our relationship is glorious and so loving. Our life is wonderful and magnificent.

339. Fulfillment
You have fulfilled all of my hopes, dreams, and expectations.

340. A Promise of A More Wonderful Life
Each day is a dream come true and a promise of more wonderful life's experiences to come.

341. Looking Forward
I am looking forward to every minute of our future which is filled with possibilities that we will share.

342. Adventure
Each day is a beautiful adventure that becomes a precious memory.

343. Boundless Love
Our love is boundless and has made us one.

344. Enormous Energy
There was an enormous amount of energy at our first meeting. The air was alive with lightning and that power was released when we first kissed.

345. Dance of Harmony
The vibrations you generate cause me to join you in a dance of harmony.

346. Utopia
You are my link between heaven and earth, and have created a utopia for me within your arms.

347. Tangible Expression
The most tangible expression I can profess is, I love you dearly and thank you for sharing your love so deeply with me.

348. Irresistible
You fill me with simple pleasures and irresistible reading challenges that expand my mind.

349. Satisfy My Hunger
You satisfy my hunger for love and give me inner peace.

350. Commitment and Honor
My life is abundant with joy and harmony. We live a poetic life that is filled with commitment and honor. I love the many ways you express your love for me.

351. Luminous With Love
My inner being is luminous with love for you, and that glow is providing me with warmth and contentment.

352. Custody of My Well Being
I grant you complete custody of my well-being, my happiness, and my joy. I love you dearly, and that love is everlasting.

353. Instrument of My Love
You are the instrument of my illumination causing me to radiate my light with greater intensity than ever before in my life.

354. Enlighten
You enlighten my entire countenance, encourage and elevate my being to a higher and higher level of vibration. You are glorious in my eyes, beautiful and resplendent.

355. Forged A Pathway
You have forged a pathway into a marvelous future that is like a reward for good behavior.

356. Respite in Your Arms
I come home at the end of a day and immediately I sense a respite from the day's rigors. I love you very much and value each and every day we have together.

357. Hunger for Love
You satisfy my hunger for love and give me inner peace. My life is abundant with joy and harmony.

358. Sealed With A Kiss
Our union is sealed with affectionate kisses, happy hugs, satisfying squeezes, romantic lovemaking, and the blissful afterglow.

359. We Tickle and Laugh
We tickle, we laugh, we discuss, we share, and we listen.

360. Dynamic Lover
You are a dynamic and enthusiastic lover, and I love the way you love me.

361. Star-Filled and Glorious
Every day with you is a day of sunshine, and every night is star-filled and glorious.

362. What I Like
What I like, you like, and what I love, you love. We live and love so harmoniously.

363. Restored Harmony to My Life
You have restored harmony to my life, and you molded a template of performance that pleasures me so.

364. New Perspective
My life has assumed a whole new perspective since you have become a part of it.

365. Important Treasure
You are the love of my life, and the most important treasure that I have.

366. Twists and Turns
The twists and turns of choices and fate have united us, and I have never been happier.

Section 2

Additional Love Messages for
Inspiration in Writing Your Own
LovE-mails

367. Grand Life
You have inspired me to abandon my solitude for the grand life that we enjoy together.

368. Blessing
Every moment we are together is a blessing, and filled with romance, intimacy, contentment, and loving.

369. Body, Mind, and Spirit
You delight my mind, my body, my spirit, and you make me whole.

370. Devoutly In Love
I am devoutly in love with you, dearly and deeply, and find enormous pleasure in our union.

371. Longing
I hear the whispers of longing when we are apart, and the time clock within me begins to count the hours, the minutes, the seconds until we are reunited.

372. Very Happy
You make me so very happy, and there is not a moment I would change from first we met to this morning's hug and kiss.

373. Bodies Joined
When our bodies joined and we discovered that the pulsating, thrilling rhythms we generated together were in accord, the second level of vibrations were found to be marvelously compatible.

374. Language of the Soul
We have learned that we share the highest level of vibration—that of the language of the soul.

375. All of My Vibrations
You delight all of my vibrations, the languages of my mind, my body, and my soul.

376. Immediately Felt Peace
Your love rushed in, and I immediately felt peace and contentment. You are the love of my life.

377. Alter My Life's Course
I never imagined that a decision to alter the course of my life so dramatically could bring me such tremendous happiness and inner harmony.

378. Motivation Behind the Impulse
You are the motivation behind the creative impulse that I embrace when sitting at my computer writing to you and thinking of all the wonderful moments we have shared and the moments to be anticipated.

379. Encoded to Match
It is as if my genetic make-up was encoded to match the balance you have brought to my life, the harmony we share, and the preservation of my spirit that you nurture every day.

380. Cuddles and Caresses
The strokes, the cuddles, the caresses, the indulgences, and the pampering all speak of your unconditional love for me, and I hope that I can reciprocate so that you know within yourself that I love you dearly.

381. Enchanted
You make our life enchanted, fulfilling, always upbeat, positive, and filled with so much love.

382. Trajectory Altered
The trajectory of my life was completely altered when first we met. I discovered that by listening to my heart and trusting my instincts, I could have a magnificent life beyond my most far-reaching dreams.

383. Surround Us
Positive energy continues to surround us, causing us to experience incredible joy, peace, and harmony.

384. Paradise
You bring me to new heights of paradise with your love, beautiful thoughts, and affirmations. I love the way you love me and I love loving you.

385. Make My Heart Full
You make my heart full and you delight all of my senses. You challenge and fulfill me intellectually. You cause me to smile inside and out and to experience extreme joy and contentment.

386. Wholeness
Your arrival home each day brings wholeness, peace, and contentment to my inner and outer worlds. I love you with all my heart and soul.

387. Realization of My Dream
I recognized very quickly that you were the realization of my dream of the perfect husband, soul mate, partner, and lover. I'm so grateful that I realized this immediately, because our life is magical and enchanting, and we are now one.

388. Time Seems to Be Suspended
Time seems to be suspended when we are together. Within your love is my heart's final destination, and here my soul finds happiness. I will love you eternally.

389. Valued and Cherished
Know that you are adored, valued, cherished, and respected. I loved you from the moment of our first kiss.

390. Sinking of the Sun
The sinking of the sun bringing on the hushed silence of night replenishes the deep feelings of love that I have for you.

391. Heat of Each Other's Bodies
As the light and warmth disappear outdoors, our light and warmth are just beginning to express themselves indoors. We hug and feel the heat of each other's bodies; we light the candles to further kindle the brightness within ourselves for one another

392. Emerging Stars
As we have wished upon the emerging stars and vowed our love as we extinguish our candles, I pray for longevity of our union and the blessings of good health. I love you deeply and thank you for all the sunshine you have brought into my life.

393. Wants and Wishes
My love for you wants, wishes, and wills nothing less than to give you unconditional happiness, harmony, and love.

394. Eternally Grateful
You are so precious to me, and I am eternally grateful to the forces that brought us together. You are an awesome partner, so giving, so sharing, so caring, and so loving.

395. Joyous Am I
What you have done to transform my life has been awesome. You are awesome. Joyous am I when you are in my arms and I feel you against me. I love you completely and dedicate my life to making you happy and to making you always feel loved and cherished.

396. Calmed the Winds of Loneliness
You have calmed the winds of loneliness by your love and devotion to me.

I am blessed to have you in my life. Thank you for loving me.

397. Perfect As You
In my pursuit of someone wonderful to be with, my expectations of finding someone as fabulous and perfect as you, were grossly underestimated.

398. Miracle of Our Meeting
Hardly a day goes by that we don't marvel about the miracle of our meeting and discuss the significant effect that our meeting has had on our love, contentment, and joy.

399. Synchronicity
We recognize and appreciate the synchronicity and forces that were at play in connecting us in that cubic centimeter of opportunity, and, as a result, we marvel and celebrate our meeting constantly.

400. Outward Expressions of Love

My outward expression of love for you is matched by my deep inner desire to please you and make you eternally aware of my love for you.

About the Authors

Marge Christensen Gould

Marge, an educator of over 28 years' experience, teaches and coordinates a highly successful program for at-risk high school students to develop literacy and workplace skills. Programs based on her model are now in existence in 10 other states. She has received several awards for teaching excellence, and was named to the All USA First Teacher Team 2000, honoring the top 20 teachers in the nation, (sponsored by *USA Today*). She has a Master's degree, and is the author of three books, a case study, and several articles. Marge is president of Educational ReadSources, a non-profit corporation which offers training for educators to implement effective classroom reform. Prior to meeting Herman she was widowed after over many years of marriage.

Herman Gould

Herman is a Doctor of Optometry with 40 years in practice, which includes teaching at the Illinois College of Optometry , and practicing for a time specializing in children's vision and vision therapy. He was a vision consultant to the Arizona State School for the Mentally Retarded and Physically Handicapped and to the Phoenix Day School for the Deaf. Herman is a member of the Board of Directors of Educational ReadSources and has written articles for educators on vision and reading, and has conducted seminars for educators. Prior to meeting Marge, he was divorced after many years of marriage.

Herman and Marge met on America Online, and have been sending one another LovE-mail messages daily ever since. They live in Tucson, AZ and have 5 children and 4 grandchildren.

www.ingramcontent.com/pod-product-compliance
Lightning Source LLC
Chambersburg PA
CBHW020252290526
45784CB00003B/1208